DODD, MEAD WONDERS BOOKS include WONDERS OF:

WONDERS OF COYOTES

Sigmund A. Lavine
Illustrated with photographs, old prints, and drawings

DODD, MEAD & COMPANY
New York

Illustrations courtesy of: American Museum of Natural History, Department Library Services, photos by Ernest Harold Baynes, Neg. no. 410608, 29, Neg. no. 106942, 53, Neg. no. 410609, 69; Author's Collection, 10 *top*, 11, 36, 37; Dr. Marc Bekoff, Dept. of E.P.O. Biology, U. of Colorado, Boulder, 64, 65, 66; Colorado Division of Wildlife, *frontispiece*, 43, 70, 71; Field Museum of Natural History, Division of Photography, 40; Interior—Sport Fisheries & Wildlife, 62; Interior—Sport Fisheries & Wildlife, photo by E. P. Haddon, 45 *bottom*; Interior—Sport Fisheries & Wildlife, photo by E. R. Kalmbach, 68; Interior—Sport Fisheries & Wildlife, photo by O. J. Murie, 50; Nicholas J. Krach, photographer, 10 *bottom*, 13, 15, 30, 34, 56, 58, 59, 61, 63, 73; Maine Fish & Game Dept., photos by Bill Cross, 8, 18, 24; Maine Fish & Wildlife Dept., photo by Tom Carbone, 41; Mary Ryan Gallery, New York, N.Y., 33; National Park Service, 48; New York State Department of Environmental Conservation, John Goerg, 17; Jane O'Regan, 45 *top*, 54; Quebec Ministry of Leisure, Fish and Game, P. Bernier, photographer, 46; Smithsonian Institution, 22–23, 27; U.S.D.A. Photograph, 75, 76.

Frontispiece: Coyote pup exploring

1 2 3 4 5 6 7 8 9 10

Library of Congress Cataloging in Publication Data

Lavine, Sigmund A.
  Wonders of coyotes.

  Includes index.
  Summary: Discusses the physical characteristics,
habits, and behavior of coyotes, as well as some of the
lore surrounding these ancient and controversial animals.
  1. Coyotes—Juvenile literature.   [1. Coyotes]
I. Title.
QL737.C22L28   1984   599.74'442   84-13798
ISBN 0-396-08464-8

To the library staff of Boston's Museum of Science,
who helped so much

CONTENTS

1

MEET THE COYOTE

Coyotes have been trotting over rolling prairies, loping through rocky desert canyons, and scrambling up wooded mountainsides in North America for a very long time. Paleontologists (experts in the identification and dating of fossils) have found well-preserved remains of an extinct species of coyote with a very thin face in the tar pits at Rancho La Brea near Los Angeles, California, one of the world's richest sources of Ice Age fossils. Painstaking study of the "record of the rocks" has also revealed that coyotes almost identical with those living today were commonplace during the Pleistocene period, which began approximately two million years ago.

Like dogs, foxes, jackals, and wolves, the coyote belongs to the family of animals known as the Canidae. Zoologists (students of animal life) refer to members of this family as canids, the scientific name for doglike animals. Paleontologists have estab-

This photo of an eastern coyote proclaims its relationship to the dog. It looks like a shepherd-collie mongrel.

9

lished that the canids and all other carnivores (meat-eaters) had common ancestors called miacids. These small carnivorous creatures lived in trees.

Certain descendants of the miacids left the trees at a very early date in order to find more prey. Larger than their forebears, with sharper claws and a bigger braincase, these long-bodied animals eventually split into two groups. One

Old print of a jackal, considered by zoologists to be the Old World equivalent of a coyote. Both animals are scavengers, omnivorous, nocturnal, and extremely vocal.

The jackal, fox, and wolf are related to the coyote. Note family resemblance as shown in a natural history published over 150 years ago. All have lithe bodies, slender legs, bushy tails, erect triangular ears, long narrow muzzles.

became the progenitor of the felines (cats). The other sired the canids.

Because of their ability to adjust to a variety of environments, the canids prospered, despite climatic changes and geological upheavals. Indeed, no kennel is large enough to hold all the doglike animals that appeared as the centuries passed. But not all of them survived the bitter cold of the Ice Age. Among those that did were the immediate ancestors of the modern coyote.

The coyote's forebears, like those of the majority of doglike animals, originated in North America. After crossing the Bering Straits by means of the land bridge that once connected present-day Alaska to Asia, many species of New World canids spread throughout Asia to Africa and Europe. However, the coyote's ancestors did not emigrate. Thus there are no coyotes in the Old World.

Nearly three hundred years before most Europeans knew that the coyote existed, this animal was a familiar sight to the conquistadors who ravaged Mexico in the early 1500's. Actually, it was a book—Francisco Javier Clavijero's *History of Mexico*, published in 1790 and translated into English from the original Italian seven years later—that introduced the coyote to Europe. But Clavijero cannot be credited with presenting the first

11

printed description of the "Coyotl or Indian Fox." This had been done in 1651 by Francisco Hernandez, a naturalist who spent several years in Mexico. Because Hernandez wrote in Latin, only a few scholars with an interest in zoology read his description of the coyote. On the other hand, Clavijero's book had a wide circulation.

Coyotl is the Aztec name for the coyote. It was adopted by the Spaniards, who substituted an *e* for the *l*. The conquistador's pronunciation of the word, "kui-outhay," eventually gave way to the Mexican version, "ki-o-tee," which crossed the border and spread through the American Southwest. In Oklahoma, as well as in Montana, Wyoming, and other northwestern states, the animal is known as the "ky-oht." Further, there are those who maintain that all three syllables in coyote should be equally accented. These individuals, however, cannot agree whether the word should be split into co-yo-te or divided into coy-o-te. No wonder J. Frank Dobie, world-famous authority on the history of the Southwest, suggests, "Perhaps there is no single right way for English-speakers to pronounce the word."

When Lewis and Clark explored the lands west of the Mississippi (1804–1806), they wrongly identified the coyotes they encountered on the Great Plains as foxes. An entry in their journal reveals that they realized their error because it describes "the small wolf or burrowing dog of the prairies." Evidently, Lewis and Clark were not sure what name they should give the coyote. In other entries in their journal, they refer to it as "wolf of the plains," "barking wolf," and "prairie wolf."

The coyote received its scientific name in 1823. In that year, Thomas Say, a biologist assigned to an expedition to the Rocky Mountains, gave it the Latin name *Canis latrans* (barking dog). While zoologists accepted Say's choice, the hardy individuals

12

Lewis and Clark mistakenly called the coyotes they encountered on the Great Plains "foxes." However, when they realized their mistake, the explorers renamed the animal "the burrowing dog of the prairies." Note that in this early picture of the Lewis and Clark expedition, Sacagawea, the Bird Woman, is leading the party with a pack on her back.

Very early printed picture of a coyote. Although it appeared thirty years after Say gave the animal its scientific name and classified it, the picture is identified as a "barking wolf." Yet the author of the book states, "all that has yet been known on this species is due to Say," showing he was familiar with the biologist's work.

Old print shows relative sizes of coyote (lower right), blue fox (upper left), red fox (upper right), and gray wolf (lower left).

who trekked west seeking their fortunes preferred to call *latrans* prairie wolf or little wolf. They had good reason. Prairie wolf distinguished the coyote from the gray or timber wolf. Little wolf indicated that *latrans* was only about one-half the size of the red wolf and approximately one-third the size of the gray wolf.

Not too long ago, coyotes lived only in the open country and grasslands of the western part of North America. Their range extended from Mexico in the south to the northern Mississippi Valley, and from eastern Wisconsin to California. Today, coyotes are found from Point Barrow, the northernmost point in Alaska, to the lush jungles of Costa Rica, throughout Canada, and from the Pacific Coast to the Atlantic Seaboard.

14

Migration came easy to *latrans*. Coyotes are natural wanderers, often traveling fifty miles in a single night. Much of this roving is in search of food. As a result, the coyote's dispersion is due in part to its hearty appetite. For example, during the cattle drives of the 1870's, it was customary to kill any calves that were born as they would slow down the herd. Drawn by this rich store of food, great numbers of scavenging coyotes followed the drives for hundreds of miles, feasting on the carcasses of the calves. Carrion was also responsible for attracting coyotes into Alaska for the first time. In 1898, during the gold rush, some prospectors attempted to pack supplies on mules and horses, but the animals were not equal to the task. Their carcasses blazed *latran's* trail into the northland.

When Texas longhorns were driven northward to the railhead, any calves born were killed so as not to slow up the herd. Coyotes followed the cattle drives to feast on the calf carcasses and, in the process, extended their range.

Food is not the only reason the coyote extended its range. Certain naturalists contend that, as the wolf was exterminated over much of the United States, coyotes moved in to fill the niche left by the larger predator. Coyotes have also been transplanted by man. Sometimes this was accidental—coyotes now native to certain areas are most likely the descendants of escaped animals once exhibited in zoos or kept as pets. Then, too, coyotes have been deliberately introduced. This undoubtedly happened in Florida, while the ancestry of Georgia's coyotes can probably be traced back to the coyotes released in that state during the early 1950's by fox hunters.

About seventy years ago, residents of the Northeast began seeing a strange, wolf-like animal—a predator that was killing both livestock and game. Because of its appearance and habits, many people thought it really was a wolf. Others maintained it was a hybrid—the offspring of a coyote and a domestic dog, and they gave it various names, the most widely accepted being "coydog."

There was good reason for thinking the newcomer was a cross between a dog and a wolf. It has long been known that coyotes and domestic dogs mate in the wild. Moreover, the characteristics of the puppies resulting from these matings have been established. During their studies of the coyote, scientists have crossbred male coyotes with female dogs and male dogs with female coyotes to determine what features the pups inherit from the parents.

As time passed, more and more sightings of the Northeast's new predator were recorded, while zoologists in the laboratory and in the field studied the animal. Eventually, their investigations and crossbreedings of dogs and coyotes confirmed that the newcomer was not a hybrid but a pure-blooded coyote. However, not only did it have slight physical differences that

Can you tell whether this is a picture of a coyote or a coydog? The photographer himself admits he isn't sure which one it is.

Like their kin living in other regions, coyotes inhabiting the Northeast are always alert. The one shown here is watching birds in a nearby tree.

distinguished it from its western kin but also it was larger and heavier. Further, the eastern coyote's variegated fur had tints that served to camouflage it in dense woods.

Establishing the identity of the eastern coyote proved a far simpler task than tracing its origins. Finally, it was theorized that the migrating coyote population, upon reaching the Great Lakes, passed into Canada and, while crossing Ontario and Quebec, bred with a local race of small wolves. The offspring of these matings continued eastward, crossed into New York State in the 1920's, and reached the New England States shortly thereafter.

While the barks and howls of the western coyote are familiar sounds in the desert and on the plains, the eastern coyote is rarely heard, having learned it is best not to call attention to itself. As a result, this coyote has prospered. It is estimated that there are at least ten thousand eastern coyotes in the State of Maine alone!

It may be that the eastern coyote is actually not a newcomer to the Northeast but a longtime resident of that region. Bounty records dating from Revolutionary times discovered in the archives of Oswego County in western New York State refer to both "big wolves" and "little wolves." Some individuals who have examined these documents believe that the "little wolves" were actually coyotes.

2

COYOTE LORE

No animal had a stronger hold on the Indian's imagination than the coyote. The ancient Aztec and Maya of Mexico, along with practically every tribe living west of the Mississippi, were convinced that the coyote had great magical powers. Proof of this is furnished by tales told in the pueblos of the Southwest, in tepees on the Great Plains, and in the brush and reed huts of the wandering Apache. These stories either credit the coyote with helping a deity create the world and prepare it for the first people or assert that the coyote single-handedly performed these miraculous deeds.

Legends of many tribes also maintain that the coyote fashioned the first humans from feathers, mud, or straw. Morever, tradition holds that, after populating the Earth, the coyote "did things that helped the people." Indeed, it would take many books the size of this one just to list the gifts the coyote supposedly presented to mankind. According to the Zuni, the coyote taught man to hunt, while the Sioux claim it instructed humans in the use of medicinal plants. In the mythology of the

Shasta and numerous other tribes, the coyote is honored for giving man fire, after stealing it from a remote and mysterious region. Another widespread legend states that the world was dismal and gloomy until the coyote took pity on the people. The Kutenay version of the coyote's kindness describes how it divided the day into equal periods of light and darkness.

While many accounts of the ways the coyote employed its wisdom and wizardry to benefit mankind are told in one form or another by several tribes, other myths are known only to a particular group of Indians. For example, stories told by the Indians of the Pacific Northwest detail how the coyote put salmon in the rivers, invented the fish trap, and made the first salmon spear. Piegan lore tells of the persecution of the "Old Ones" by evil monsters until the fiends were killed by the coyote. A Seri myth maintains that the coyote showed the tribe how to remove the spines from the juicy fruit of the cactus so that it could be eaten.

Sioux legend also credits the coyote with providing man with food. In the beginning—so the story goes—the buffalo (bison) was so keen sighted that hunters could not get close enough to shoot it with a bow and arrow. As a result, the people were starving. The coyote came to their rescue. It kicked sand into the buffalo's eyes and, from that time to this, the buffalo has been nearsighted.

When recounting creation myths featuring the coyote or telling of the animal's relationship with their ancestors, Indians call the coyote by various names. Depending upon the tribe, the wonder-working animal is known as Old Man, Old Man Coyote, Coyote Being, or a similar name. But irrespective of what name the coyote is given by tribal storytellers, it is depicted either as a supernatural being or an animal that thinks and acts like a man. Thus, many tribes, including the Navajo who feature *latrans* in their mythology, always refer to it as "Coyote."

Many Indians believed that the coyote not only taught man to hunt but also made it possible for him to kill buffalo (bison). Tribal legend holds that, when the world was young, the buffalo had such keen sight no hunter could get close to it until the coyote kicked sand in its eyes and made it nearsighted.

Beside venerating Coyote as a benefactor and a godlike creator, the Indians tell of his activities as the Transformer. In this guise, Coyote is said to have altered the course of rivers, moved mountains, dried up lakes, and otherwise remodeled the landscape. Tradition maintains that these transformations corrected mistakes made when the Earth was created. Thus

This picture of Blackfeet hunting was painted by George Catlin, who spent eight years (1832–1839) recording the activities of the Indians of the Great Plains.

the path of the sun was changed so that the people would get more light and warmth. Originally, it is believed, the heavens held several moons, but the Transformer removed all but one from the evening sky.

The Transformer, according to legend, often imposed his will on humans. When the Holy People (the ancestors of the Navajo)

23

The coyote was known to the Indians as the Trickster, the Transformer, and also the Creator. The eastern coyote pictured here in an attitude of submission was photographed in Maine.

began to set all the Earth's vegetation in orderly rows, the Transformer stopped them. He explained that such an arrangement would make it easy for enemies to destroy food crops. The Holy People agreed and scattered the seeds of plants all over the countryside. A similar story is told by the Hopi. They claim that when the Ancient Ones finally emerged into this world they decided to place the stars in the heavens in a regular pattern. The Transformer thought this was a waste of time and took the stars, flinging them upward in all directions—and so we see them today.

A Mandan myth is typical of the tales told of the Transformer's activities. According to the Mandan, dogs formerly had the power of speech and spent the day spreading gossip through the villages. Their idle chatter created friction between neighbors, and the Transformer decided to stop the bickering. He took the ability to speak away from the dogs but allowed them to bark and growl, as they still do. Coyote, the Transformer, is also credited by some tribes with changing the ways of the elk. When the first people complained that elk were feeding on human flesh, the Transformer turned the animals into grass eaters.

Perhaps the greatest gift the Transformer gave to man was the ability to think. This enabled Coyote to help mankind establish customs and ceremonies. Because of this guidance, mankind prospered, but Coyote realized that within a short time there would not be enough food to feed all the people. This is why death was introduced into the world.

The coyote takes three different forms in Indian lore. As noted, two of these are the supernatural beings, Coyote the creator and the wonder-working Transformer. In its third guise, the coyote is neither revered nor admired. In fact, the animal is considered a self-centered mischief-maker that cheats, lies, and steals in order to get what it wants. Known as the Trickster, this coyote constantly attempts to outsmart others but usually ends up looking foolish.

There are two types of Trickster stories. The first consists of single-incident accounts. Many of them describe how the vain and jealous Trickster employed deception or flattery to gain his ends. In all these tales the coyote is duped by his intended victims, despite his shrewd cunning. In fact, even such simple creatures as the rabbit and opossum expose the Trickster as a silly cheat.

Other single-incident stories explain how the coyote acquired its physical appearance. One of the most widespread of these yarns states that a sorcerer gave the Trickster the power to send his eyes vast distances and then recall them. Although warned not to do this too often, the Trickster, in hope of seeing everything that was going on in the world, constantly sent his eyes abroad. One day, unable to call them back, he became blind. The Trickster continued his dishonest ways while seeking some means of restoring his sight. Eventually, he tucked solidified sap from a pine tree into his eye sockets. This is why all coyotes have yellow eyes.

A great number of Trickster tales are rather long. Most are loosely linked together. This is because the action of each story is more or less connected to the action of the stories that precede and follow it. Generally speaking, this category of Trickster yarns is designed to amuse those who hear them. But a few illustrate the coyote's irascibility through telling a fanciful account of the origin of a mountain, lake, or other landmark. Thus Indians native to the State of Washington claim that the Trickster prevented salmon from going up the Spokane River to spawn because he was angry with the Indian's ancestors, who refused to let him marry the tribe's most beautiful girl. If you ask how the Trickster stopped the salmon, the Indians point to Spokane Falls.

26

Humor abounds in the single-incident Trickster stories. But, unlike the longer tales, they are not meant to entertain. They are designed to teach a moral lesson and to impress upon both adults and children that they must *never* act as the dishonest and wicked coyote did.

As indicated, the coyote played an important role in the redman's religion. However, the reverence in which *latrans* was held varied from tribe to tribe. Some had so little regard for the animal that they believed wrongdoers, upon reaching the Land of the Dead, were sent back to Earth as coyotes. On the other hand, the Blackfoot appealed to the coyote for help and protection in their most devout prayers. California Indians not only engaged in rites honoring the coyote but also venerated a mythical white coyote that lived beside a river flowing through the sky.

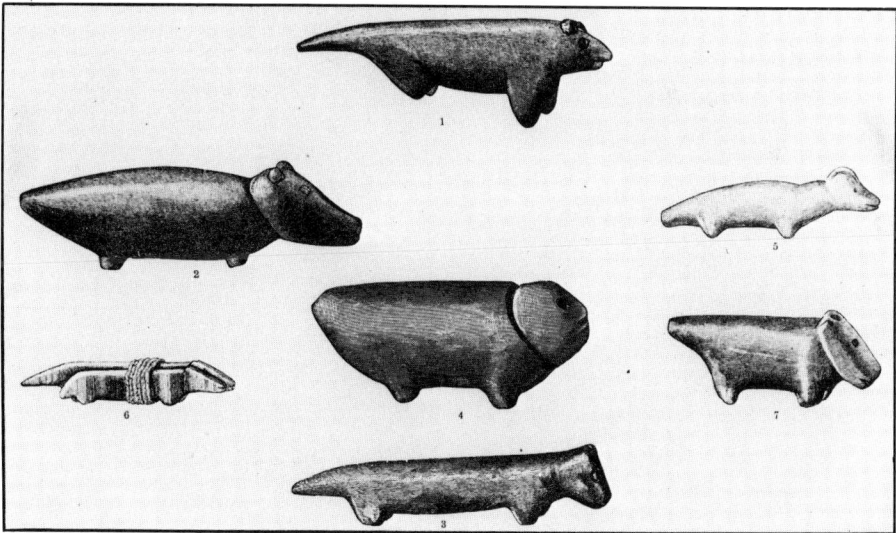

Fetishes in the form of coyotes used by Zuni shamans for successful hunts

It was widely believed that if a shaman's guardian spirit was a coyote, it appeared to him in dreams. The animal then supposedly enabled tribal wizards to communicate with the gods and also gave advice. Medicine men with exceptional magical powers were credited with being able to receive guidance from a supernatural coyote without dreaming. Followers of these shamans were convinced that by listening to the howls and yips of coyotes, their leaders could tell whether friends or enemies were approaching a village under the cover of darkness. Incidentally, the Comanche claim that at one time all the members of that tribe could converse with coyotes. They had learned the animal's language from a lost boy brought up by a family of coyotes.

Few tribes venerated the coyote more than the Aztec of Mexico. Proof of this is furnished by the presence of the word *coyotl* in the names of several Aztec gods. One of these deities was Huehuecoyotl who, like the Trickster, was a troublemaker. Coyotlinautl was a more benevolent supernatural, and his worshipers, dressed in coyote skins, held festivals in his honor. Perhaps the most aptly named of all Aztec divinities is Coyotl-auxhqui, the moon goddess—the nightly coyote chorus is loudest when the moon is full.

Tezcatlipoca, ruler of the upper air, was closely linked to the coyote by the Aztec. He was credited with watching over the affairs of men and considered most protective of humans. Thus Tezcatlipoca was thought to turn himself into a coyote in order to overtake travelers and warn them of dangers ahead.

When Cortez conquered Mexico and razed Tenochtitlan, the Aztec capital, he established the first government of New Spain in the small village of Coyoacan. Today, Coyoacan is a suburb of Mexico City and its ancient, tree-shaded streets are lined with the homes of artists and writers. While some of these individuals are world famous, much information about the

This picture was taken on a moonlit night. Note the alert expression on the coyote's face as the click of the camera catches its attention.

original inhabitants of Coyoacan is lacking. However, it is very likely that they took part in rites and rituals featuring the coyote. The translation of Coyoacan is Place-of-the-Coyote-Cult.

The Mexicans of yesteryear worshiped the coyote; their modern descendants regard it with superstitious dread. Mexican cowboys are convinced that if they ride in a coyote's tracks, their horses will stumble. Vaqueros also hold that one cannot

29

shout at a coyote—if you try, all you can do is mumble. Meanwhile, many Mexican hunters, convinced they will find no game if a coyote crosses their path, will give up the chase and return home. Incidentally, these hunters probably have hung coyote skulls around their goats' necks to protect them from predators.

A tuft of hair, claw, or small bone from a coyote is carried by the credulous to keep witches away. Yet Mexicans have always associated the coyote with black magic. In his voluminous account of life in New Spain written in 1560, Fr. Bernardino de Sahagún reports: "The animal of this country called the Coyotl is very sagacious in waylaying. When he wishes to attack, he first casts breath over the victim to stupefy it. . . . Diabolical, indeed is the creature."

Despite the coyote's link to sorcery, Mexicans on both sides of the Rio Grande claim that coyotes repay those that help them. There are dozens of "true" stories detailing how a coyote presents a chicken, rabbit, or some other gift to humans who

Many Mexicans claim that coyotes thank humans who help them by presenting a gift. They also think the coyote will take revenge on those who hurt them.

30

have released it from a trap, provided water during a drought, or killed a rattlesnake attacking coyote pups. It is just as widely held that if a coyote is mistreated, it gets revenge by haunting the individual responsible or by destroying his livestock.

It is said that coyotes can hypnotize domestic fowl and wild birds by waving their tails. Clavijero records another superstition about the coyote's tail. He writes that when a coyote seizes a sheep, it holds its victim " . . . by the neck with his teeth and, dragging it and beating on its rump with its tail, conducts it where it pleases." Although it is obvious that a coyote's bushy tail would have little impact on a sheep's thick pelt, some sheepherders still hold to this ancient belief.

Other age-old fancies about the coyote persist. Among them are the convictions that the animal can cast spells with its eyes and turn itself into a ghost no bullet can harm. Meanwhile, the Navajo exhibit mixed emotions about the coyote. Elderly members of the tribe will not kill or skin a sheep-eating coyote because they hold that coyotes are the spirits of the dead. Young Navajos are apt to shoot or trap coyotes that prey upon their sheep. However, like their ancestors, those who ignore the old ways still call the coyote "God's Dog."

In both Mexico and the American Southwest, common speech has been enriched by the coyote. Along the border, the dishonest individuals who smuggle aliens into the United States are known as coyotes. So are the lawyers in Texas who overcharge ignorant migrant workers for minor services. Mexicans also refer to petty thieves and swindlers as coyotes and say a group of people who shout at one another instead of calmly discussing their differences is a *coyotera*. In New Mexico, coyote is the slang term for a person of mixed ancestry. Throughout the Southwest, anyone who has little to do with his neighbors is classified as a "lone coyote."

Americans who take pride in being labeled "foxy" resent being called a coyote or told they are "as smart as a coyote." However, outdoorsmen are flattered when credited with "coyote sense"—it means that they can find their way over trackless desert or through thick woods. But no compliment is intended when an individual is likened to a cowardly coyote, a sneaking coyote, or a dirty coyote.

When the Mormons first settled Utah, they lived in dirt cellars roofed with boards. These temporary shelters were called "coyote houses" because they were underground. Meanwhile, in the California gold fields, shafts sunk in canyon walls were known as "coyote diggings," a blast inside a chamber was referred to as a "coyote blast," while anyone who operated a small claim was said to be "coyoteing around." In the Southwest today, "coyoteing around" infers that an individual avoids responsibility by drifting from job to job.

Even a casual glance at an atlas reveals that the coyote has given its name to hundreds of canyons, mesas, mountains, streams, and other physical features of the landscape in North and Central America. Moreover, a goodly number of modern communities owe their names to the coyote. Perhaps the best known is Prairie du Chien in Wisconsin. Established about 1751 by the French, the settlement was given its present name because of the many coyotes that lived nearby.

The numerous coyotes that once ranged its rolling plains are responsible for South Dakota's nickname—the Coyote State. Moreover, the athletic teams of the University of South Dakota are known to their fans as the Coyotes. This designation is also applied to the teams of several other institutions of higher learning located in Idaho, Kansas, and Texas.

There are dozens of proverbs featuring the coyote. When a Mexican declares, "The coyote won't get another chicken from me," it means the speaker has learned an expensive lesson.

"The Plainsman" depicted in this lithograph by John Stuart Curry is typical of the hunters and trappers who gave names to many places throughout the West and also adopted the Indians' superstitions about the coyote. Because of these outlandish beliefs, most early accounts of the habits of latrans *are fantastic rather than factual.*

Those who own valuable property or have a beautiful daughter are warned, "Whoever has chickens must watch for coyotes." On both sides of the Rio Grande, "He has heard the coyote bark" means that an individual has been everywhere and seen everything.

Strangely enough, the coyote is treated as a rather stupid creature in Central American folklore, although it supposedly has the power to cause the gates of enclosed pastures to swing open. One Mexican proverb pays the coyote a compliment— in fact, no higher praise is possible than "Next to God the coyote is the smartest person on Earth."

33

Many Indian tribes believed that the coyote controlled the weather. Certain of them held that, because the coyote was the offspring of the sun and moon, it had the power to make a day hot and dry or cold and wet. Other tribes explained the changing seasons by telling of a race between Coyote and Cloud when the world was young. The winner of the race was to decide the weather, Cloud wanting it to be stormy, Coyote insisting that every day be pleasant. Cloud would have lost the race if he had not caused fruit-laden bushes to spring up in Coyote's path. Coyote stopped to eat the fruit and Cloud was the first to cross the finish line. This, the Indians maintain, is why we have winter.

The coyote is featured in hundreds of legends and proverbs, as well as weather lore.

Today, ranchers and farmers claim that "When coyotes wail it is going to rain and when they shout it will be dry." It is also widely believed that if coyotes howl after the sun rises it will rain: the higher the animals howl, the greater the downpour. If coyotes yip—so it is said—the weather will be fair, but if they bark in deep tones it will be stormy. When coyotes "sing" more than usual during a dry spell, it is a sign of prolonged drought.

Rural residents of the Great Plains have long relied upon the howls of coyotes to warn them of worsening weather. The American novelist Willa Cather writes of this forecasting in *My Ántonia*, " . . . between the blasts the coyotes tuned up their whining one, two, three, then all together—to tell us snow was coming."

Relatively few people have heard the Seri chant their coyote song but thousands are familiar with two American folk songs that feature the coyote: The "Old Chisolm Trail" and "Bury Me Not on the Lone Prairie." The latter ballad was so popular in the 1880's that there was "a saying on the range that even horses nickered it and the coyotes sang it."

Literature has not neglected the coyote. It lopes through countless stories both true and fictional. The coyote has also appealed to poets. Those who have been inspired by *latrans* include Robert Van Carr, Peter Blue Cloud, A. A. Dowling, Bret Harte, Gwendolen Hate, Leslie Siko, and the unknown Zuni tribesman who produced "The Coyote and the Locust," a prose poem that has been beautifully translated into English by Frank Hamilton Cushing.

Perhaps the kindest coyotes in literature are the ones that found a baby who had fallen out of a covered wagon crossing the Texas plains. The animals took the infant to their den and raised it with their pups. Eventually the youngster became the leader of all the coyotes in Texas but left his foster parents to work on a ranch. Known from the Rio Grande to the Panhandle as Pecos Bill, he not only became the most famous of cowboys and the inventor of the six-shooter but also is credited with teaching broncos to buck.

The first known appearance of *latrans* in art dates back to the Aztec Empire when skilled craftsmen carved these animals out of solid rock and incised the hieroglyphic symbols representing them on the walls of public buildings.

One of the best depictions of the coyote is the work of John J. Audubon, the internationally famous naturalist/painter who

John James Audubon was not only one of the first to study and paint the birds of the United States but also to wander far and wide sketching animals. This picture of the "prairie wolf" was drawn by Audubon for his famous The Viviparous Quadrupeds of North America.

Frederic Remington, famous American artist who worked as a cowboy throughout the Old West, drew this picture for Harper's Weekly *in 1890 while visiting a military post in California. The chase depicted here is almost over as the greyhounds surround the coyote.*

observed and sketched *latrans* on the prairies in the early nineteenth century. Other realistically drawn coyotes appear in natural history books illustrated by Friedrich Specht and J. Mutzell that were published a century ago.

Art critics praise "Coyotes," a modern painting by Clayton S. Price. However, laymen are apt to prefer Charles Marion Russell's lively drawings of cowboys roping coyotes or Frederic Remington's "Waiting for a Chinook." Equally pleasing are the sketches made by Adolph Murie of the United States Park Service. (See page 48.)

"It is a strange beast that hath neither head nor tail."
—DRAKE

3
PHYSICAL CHARACTERISTICS

Zoologists have classified nineteen subspecies of coyotes. Some have extended ranges. Others are confined to a limited area. *Canis latrans* (as noted, Say gave this name to the plains coyote) is the most widespread of them all. It thrives in diverse habitats. On the other hand, Mearn's coyote (*Canis latrans mearnsi*) is found only on Tiburon Island off the northwest coast of Mexico.

Certain of the physical differences between the subspecies stem from the type of habitat each occupies. For example, coyotes native to wooded regions tend to have dark fur, which makes them difficult to see in the underbrush. Similarly, the tawny coats of desert-dwelling coyotes blend with sand and weathered rock. Geography is also responsible for variations in the texture of the fur. Subspecies living in colder areas have coarser fur.

Not only does habitat determine what type of fur coat a

subspecies will wear but also it influences an animal's size and weight. Coyotes living where they have little or no difficulty securing food are bigger and heavier than coyotes forced to range far and wide to satisfy their appetites.

It is a relatively simple task to distinguish some subspecies of coyotes from others. Even a casual observer can note the difference in size between the mountain coyote (*Canis latrans lestes*) and Mearn's coyote. *Lestes* can weigh as much as seventy pounds, while Mearn's coyote rarely weighs more than twenty pounds. However, only experts are able to identify positively certain small subspecies—this because the only distinction between one subspecies and another may be the slightest variation in the shape of the skull. In some instances, dissection in the laboratory is necessary to detect the minor cranial differences.

Irrespective of diversity in coloration, size, and weight, all subspecies of coyotes closely resemble one another. Therefore, in the pages that follow, unless special attention is called to a dissimilarity, it is to be understood that the physical characteristic being discussed is identical in all nineteen subspecies.

General Appearance

At first glance, a coyote looks like a medium-sized dog of mixed shepherd-collie ancestry. Not only is this resemblance enhanced by *latrans'* coloration but also it is strengthened by the similarity between the size and weight of the average shepherd-collie mongrel and the average coyote.

Coyotes stand from fifteen to twenty-four inches high at the shoulder. The maximum length of the body—including the cylindrical eleven- to sixteen-inch tail—is about four feet. Adult males are usually heavier than fully grown females. Field observations and laboratory investigations have revealed that the northern subspecies, as well as those subspecies inhabiting

In large cities throughout the United States, coyotes thrive. Few people can readily identify these animals—after all, doesn't this coyote resemble a friendly German shepherd?

Rumors of extremely large and heavy eastern coyotes are common. To determine the average size of coyotes living in Maine, wildlife biologists measure and weigh as many as they can.

higher elevations, tend to be considerably larger than subspecies living in lowlands and in warm areas. As noted, the so-called eastern coyote is also larger than its western kin.

The largest recorded coyote, weighing almost seventy-five pounds, was taken in Wyoming. Although other coyotes weighing fifty pounds or more have been shot or trapped elsewhere, such oversized individuals are not common. The average weight of coyotes belonging to all nineteen subspecies is between twenty-two and twenty-five pounds. However, because *latrans* has extremely thick fur, even the thinnest and most narrow-chested specimens give the impression of being much larger than they actually are.

Fur

Although, as indicated, the fur of coyotes living in different habitats varies in color, the pelts of all coyotes are some shade of gray enlivened with highlights of brown, red, or yellow. Irrespective of its hue, the fur of all coyotes is coarse, grizzled, rough, and rather long. While the coloration of both sexes is

41

identical, there is a wide range of tints in the coats of individuals belonging to the same subspecies. As a result, it is impossible to set down a single description of the animal's fur that would include all of the colorations recorded. As an example, some coyotes have light fur, others wear dark coats. Still others have blotches of color on the backs and flanks or carry a white stripe across the shoulders. Then, too, specimens with rufous-red pelts similar to that of the red fox are common. So are those with coats of a distinct bluish or yellowish cast. Pure white and totally black coyotes are known but they are quite rare.

Despite the variations in the fur of both subspecies and individuals of the same subspecies, the gray or tawny upperparts of a typical coyote contain numerous black hairs. In certain specimens, the black is more pronounced down the middle of the back, which adds a most attractive accent to the pelt. Normally, this deep color is carried to the tail, which is touched with black at the base and tip. Underparts may be buffy, pale yellow, or whitish. The rusty or yellowish legs bear a vertical line on the forearm. White splotches the face; the upper lip is also whitish, contrasting with the black muzzle.

Like its western kin, the eastern coyote wears a fur coat of many different colors. Long hairs over the shoulders form a "cape" more pronounced than that of the western species. Characteristically, the dark stripes down the forearms end in dark spots on the toes of the front feet.

Coyote fur undergoes seasonal changes. In cold regions, it becomes thicker with the approach of winter. In midwinter, the pelt is at its brightest. This winter coat, which serves as an insulation blanket, is composed of the short, soft underfur and longer and coarser guard hairs that are tipped with black. The long guard hairs provide a protective shield for the underfur and, as is to be expected, the further north a subspecies lives, the longer and thicker its guard hairs. During the winter when

In full winter pelage, this western coyote scans the Colorado countryside, looking for possible danger.

blizzards sweep across the Great Plains, prairie coyotes "look like fur barrels." Conversely, during the summer, the pelage of coyotes native to warm regions is composed of short bristles.

Subspecies inhabiting colder regions wear their winter coats for a considerably longer time than do subspecies in warmer areas. However, all coyotes have started to shed by late spring. Before the shedding begins, the prime winter coat has faded. The overhair is shed first, the molt starting at the base of the tail, then moving up the sides and back. This gives *latrans* a mangy look. When the summer coat grows in, it is much shorter than the winter pelt.

Although the Indians used coyote fur to make clothing, trappers showed little interest in *latrans'* pelage until the late 1860's, when coyote fur became a fashionable trim for coats. Some time later, furriers, finding coyote fur easy to dye, marketed it under the name "imitation fox." However, coyote fur was never really popular, although it sold well in the 1930's as "coonskin." At that time, a prime pelt was worth only a few dollars. The development of synthetic "fun furs" further depressed the value of coyote pelts until recently. Today, a full-length coat made of selected coyote skins costs between twenty-five hundred and five thousand dollars.

Legs

Latrans' agile, graceful body is supported by long slender legs that are thinner than the legs of most dogs. Coyote feet are also smaller than those of dogs of comparative size. The front feet have five toes, the hind only four. All toes bear rather blunt, nonretractile claws that usually leave their imprint in their tracks. The size of coyote tracks vary, depending upon the subspecies. The tracks of females are more pointed and smaller than those of males. In all subspecies, the hind print is slightly narrower and smaller than the fore print. Generally

Coyotes have four toes on the hind feet, five on the front. Unlike cats, coyotes cannot retract their claws.

speaking, a male coyote's tracks are approximately two-and-a-half inches long and an inch-and-a-half wide.

While the strides of the various subspecies differ, the distance between the imprints of the fore and hind feet of a walking coyote is about thirteen inches. When a coyote trots, the tracks are two feet apart. A running coyote's tracks are separated by thirty inches or more.

Coyotes can cover thirteen miles in an hour when walking. If they trot—their favorite gait—they average twenty miles an hour for long periods. *Latrans'* top speed is thirty miles an hour, which is reached during galloping. Individual coyotes

Coyote striding through grass on the flats of southeastern Colorado

To avoid being trapped in deep snow, coyotes carefully test the strength of the crust to make sure it can support them. Moving slowly forward, placing one foot behind another, the animals immediately shift their weight in another direction if a paw breaks through.

often attain speeds far greater than these averages—one specimen was clocked at forty-three miles an hour. Running at top speed, a coyote skims over the ground, "legs working like short pistons, the ears laid back on the outstretched head, and the tail streaming behind."

Although their powerful legs enable coyotes to leap a distance of fourteen feet, clear a four-foot fence, and swim in fast-moving waters, the animals have difficulty moving through deep snow. To avoid breaking through the crust that covers the snow pack, coyotes constantly test its thickness with their front paws. When convinced that the crust will support their weight, they advance cautiously, placing one foot in front of another. If a front paw

46

pierces the crust, coyotes immediately attempt to shift their weight in another direction. This maneuver is not always successful and the coyote becomes mired in snow. While floundering, it may be fortunate enough to regain a foothold and clamber to safety or find the strength to plow to a spot the wind has blown clear of snow. But, all too often, coyotes trapped in snow die lingering deaths.

Head

As indicated, slight variations in the shape of the skull distinguish certain subspecies. Nevertheless, all coyotes have slender and relatively short skulls that broaden in front of the eyes. The eyes themselves have dark, round pupils and a yellow iris.

Long, narrow, pointed muzzles are characteristic of all coyotes, that of the eastern coyote being less pointed than those of its kin, while the nose pad is wider. All nineteen subspecies also have pointed, erect, fur-covered ears that are movable although directed forward. Like its tail, the eastern coyote's ears are rather shorter than those of other coyotes.

Coyotes have forty-two teeth set in extremely strong jaws that are capable of crushing large bones. Coyotes' canines (tearing teeth) are relatively long, recurving, sharp, and pointed. These formidable weapons bring down deer and other large prey. When eating, *latrans'* carnassial teeth (certain teeth that are larger and longer than adjacent teeth) act like shears and cut away large chunks of flesh, which are gulped down without chewing.

Senses

Years ago, so legend claims, a Yosemite chief wrapped his newborn son in a coyote skin in hopes that the boy would magically acquire *latrans'* acute hearing, keen eyesight, and

47

Something stirring!

O. J. Murie, an employee of the National Park Service and a pioneer student of the life history and habits of the coyote, drew these pictures during his studies of latrans in Yellowstone Park. Originally, Murie believed that coyotes were harmful predators but his investigations taught him that they were actually friends of man.

A mouse?

The pounce

strong sense of smell. Modern naturalists appreciate the chief's action. They know that very few animals have sharper eyes or more sensitive ears and nose than the coyote.

Latrans employs its outer ears as antennae. They are twitched forward and back in order to pinpoint the direction from which a sound is coming. Even the faint noise made by semidormant meadow mice wintering in the narrow tunnel of air that floats between the ground and hard-packed snow is detected by hunting coyotes.

Because of their excellent hearing, coyotes can communicate with one another by wailing or howling, even though far apart. *Latrans* may respond to the sounds made by other creatures, including man, or ignore them. If an individual feels secure, it may pay no attention to what it hears but usually there is an immediate reaction. For example, when adult coyotes are hunting, their unattended pups waste no time in seeking the safety of the den if they hear the warning cry of a raven.

Ever since the days of the mountain men, hunters and trappers have maintained that coyotes can see humans long before humans see them. *Latrans* is also credited with having such sharp eyes that it can tell whether or not a person is carrying a gun. This may or may not be true. However there is no doubt that coyotes have excellent sight.

Yet, strangely enough, *latrans* is apt to pay very little attention to nearby stationary objects even if they are potentially dangerous. On the other hand, the slightest movement seen yards away will provoke a prompt response. Incidentally, while coyotes' eyes are adapted for seeing in dim light, the color vision of all subspecies is quite limited.

Coyotes rely on their eyes not only to spot prey but also to inform them that a feast of carrion is available. The animals scan the sky from time to time, looking for flocks of scavenger birds hovering in the air. When they see such a flock, they get

Latrans *can hear the faintest stirring of meadow mice under the snow.*

to it as fast as possible, instinctively knowing the birds have found a carcass.

While carrying out their daily routine, coyotes depend upon olfactory clues to a great extent. For example, they mark the limits of their territories with urine and feces to warn intruders against trespassing. Similarly, any coyotes that venture into an established territory leave their "marks" at its boundaries. As a result, the rightful owner of a territory is warned that he has uninvited visitors. An oval gland near the base of the tail exudes each animal's individual scent, which is recognized by other coyotes.

Although *latrans* has the ability to detect faint odors, strong ones have a peculiar fascination for all coyotes. Thus traps baited with powder puffs filled with inexpensive facial powder or saturated with cheap perfume, urine, or foul-smelling chemicals have caught many a coyote. Besides being attracted to unusual scents, which they sniff with obvious pleasure, coyotes also delight in rolling on putrid carcasses or other objects that stink.

Some zoologists debate whether *latrans'* sense of smell is more acute than its eyesight. However, many authorities agree with naturalist Joseph Grinnell, who maintains, "I do not believe that the coyote's sense of smell is notably keener than its sense of sight. Observations made with binoculars have shown that a coyote stalking meadow mice in an aspen meadow depends more on its sense of hearing to guide it to its prey."

Voice

With the exception of the domestic dog, the coyote is the only canid that habitually barks. But *latrans'* vocal cords are not limited to producing various barks. As a matter of fact, opera singers have good reason to envy the coyote's repertoire. Not only can it "sing" bass, soprano, or tenor but also it has a long list of calls, which have been recorded by Dr. Phillip N. Lehner, a biologist working at Colorado State University. Dr. Lehner established that *latrans* can growl, huff, whine, yelp, woof, bark, bark-woof, lone howl, group howl, and group howl-yip, and has a greeting song as well. Moreover, the "Voice of the Desert" can combine certain growls, howls, wails, and yaps by raising or lowering its voice. Coyotes, which may be the most musical of all land mammals, have a range of at least two octaves when howling.

Whether heard in a desert canyon, on the rolling prairie, or in wooded country, the wail of the coyote has a haunting quality. It is usually heard as dusk falls, during the night, or as dawn brightens the sky. Most coyote concerts begin with a drawn-out, quavering, mournful wail "that seems to rise to the stars beyond." One field naturalist has described this prelude as "a prolonged howl which the animal lets out and then runs after it and bites into small pieces." The introductory wail ends as suddenly as it begins in a series of yaps and yips.

Usually when a coyote lifts its nose skyward and starts to sing, every other coyote within hearing distance answers the soloist in a countermelody of howls, wails, and yaps. Before long, still other coyotes farther away from the first singer join the swelling chorus. Coyotes sing with so much gusto that a family group of three or four individuals originating a songfest sound as if at least a dozen animals were taking part.

As they sing, coyotes give the impression that they are constantly shifting their position. At times they appear to be quite near. A minute later, the singers seem to be at least a mile away. But coyotes are not phantoms of the night. Actually, these animals are master ventriloquists. However, they do not have as much skill in "throwing" their voices as they were credited with by early settlers of the Old West. These pioneers claimed that coyotes gave the impression they were a distance away by barking into rodent holes in order to create a hollow echo. Then, too, old-time trappers maintained that coyotes could not produce their lingering howls unless their chests were vibrating. According to the trappers, the animals made their chests vibrate by jumping up and down on stiff hind legs!

Coyotes do not use their voices merely for singing. When physically separated, mated coyotes keep in touch with one another by howling. Field observation has revealed that coyotes recognize each other's voices over long distances. This enables them to employ vocalization to send information about possible danger, the discovery of a source of food, or to ask for help. Listening to coyotes has convinced most naturalists that "coyotes often howl for the pure pleasure of it and, that at times, they howl because they are lonely."

The coyote emits a mournful wail that seems "to rise to the stars beyond."
This one sitting in the snow displays its teeth as it sings.

The ability to vocalize is important to the coyote.

Vocalization plays a part in coyote courtship. It is also very important in the rearing and training of young. Hunting parents keep in touch with their offspring by both sight and voice. Incidentally, although coyote pups raised in captivity as pets learn to howl spontaneously, pups in the wild have been seen taking singing lessons from their parents.

All subspecies of coyotes speak the same "language." This was confirmed by Hope Ryden, a leading authority on the life history and behavior of *latrans*. She played a tape of a female prairie coyote calling her pups for a litter of coydogs raised in captivity by a zoologist in New Hampshire. At the same place in the tape where the female's pups had tumbled helter-skelter into their parent's den on the plains of Wyoming, the little New Hampshire coydogs dashed to the shelter of their kennel.

54

*"They say that the first inclination which an animal has is
to protect itself."*
—DIOGENES

4

WAYS OF THE COYOTE

No predator has a keener instinct for survival than the coyote. Thus, although extremely curious, *latrans* is always wary when investigating anything unfamiliar. Most coyotes will flee immediately if they sense danger while exploring. But some are bold as well as cunning. Actually there is as much deviation in the behavior of individual coyotes as there is in their coloration.

Temperament

Despite the claims of those who would exterminate it, the coyote is not a vicious animal. To be sure, males fight over potential mates, family groups defend their kills from strangers, and pups battle for dominance. However, *latrans*, unlike some canids, does not depend primarily on tooth and claw to survive. Intelligent, it attempts to outsmart all its enemies, including man.

General and Mrs. George Armstrong Custer playing with the pets of the famous Seventh Cavalry. According to an 1867 newspaper report, the troops owned ". . . four pretty little antelopes and eight young wolves, principally of the coyote kind, which are something of a menagerie in themselves. But add to this eagles, ravens, prairie-dogs, jack-rabbits with ears twenty-three inches from tip to tip, an owl or two and some fangless rattlesnakes, and the reader will have some idea of the pets in camp."

Because coyotes are independent, high spirited, and very nervous, they rarely make satisfactory pets. However, some coyotes do develop a deep affection for humans. These individuals, like their wild kin, are unpredictable. One may try to help its owner's dog raise a litter of pups but kill the household cat.

Observers have seen coyotes "dancing," playing with birds, and engaging in other seemingly foolish antics. Indeed, *latrans* appears to have a sense of humor, although scientists avoid crediting animals with human characteristics. Nevertheless, Mary Austin, an American author who wrote chiefly on Indian life in the Southwest, nicknamed the coyote "the Charlie Chaplin of the Plains." Erle Stanley Gardner, the famous mystery story writer, also maintained that coyotes are fun loving. He told how his pet coyote delighted in stealing the bedding from under a big, sleeping dog. Chased by the much larger dog, the coyote would stuff the bedding underneath a low couch where the dog could not get at it.

Diet

Although carnivores, coyotes eat a large amount of vegetation. Indeed, at certain seasons in some areas, their menu consists of berries, fruit, and grasses. Coyotes will always dine on what is most readily obtainable, whether or not they prefer some other food. Opportunistic feeders, they will swallow anything, whether it is edible or not. Some of the items *latrans* gulps down are indeed unusual. String, paper, cloth, part of an automobile tire, harness buckles, and porcupine quills are among the objects that have been found in their stomachs.

Because *latrans* is a predator attacking both game and livestock, biologists seeking to learn as much as possible about its feeding habits have examined the stomach contents of thousands of these canids. The investigations have revealed that, although menus vary geographically, the main dishes are rabbits, rodents, insects, and fish. During the winter months, *latrans* feasts on far more carrion than in the summer. Coyotes are avid scavengers and will steal a "free lunch" from carcasses cached by other predators. However, they are apt to shy away from robbing a mountain lion's fresh kill.

If coyotes acquire more than enough food to satisfy their ravenous appetites, they bury the excess for future use. The

George Catlin drew this picture of a prairie dog community. Although the artist writes he was forced to ride several miles out of his way to get by it, this was a small "town." A colony of prairie dogs in Texas was 250 miles long and 100 miles wide. Coyotes that lived nearby ate well!

Before the prairies were turned into ranches and farms, vast communities of prairie dogs lived on the Great Plains. In those days, the gregarious prairie dog, which resembles "a very fat rat with a short tail," was a staple food for the coyote. Today, prairie dogs are not numerous, and field mice and other rodents have become more important in latrans' diet.

Coyotes have learned that it is almost impossible for them to overcome a beaver when it is in the water. Therefore, although latrans *will plunge into a river or pond to dine on fish or frogs, it will never try to feast on beaver meat unless the beaver is on land.*

kind of food eaten determines the need for water. Individuals feeding on fresh kills require very little. Adult coyotes rearing pups usually drink once every twenty-four hours. In warm weather, the coyote's need for water increases. This is particularly true in the dry Southwest, where desert-dwelling coyotes display an uncanny ability to find water in the desert, often digging two to three feet in the sand. These "coyote wells" have saved many a prospector's life.

To vary its menu, *latrans* will plunge into water to capture crayfish, frogs, tadpoles, and turtles. The coyote also has a taste for watermelons, always finding the ripest and juiciest ones in the patch.

Hunting

Latrans' appetite, like its curiosity, is insatiable. Therefore coyotes spend most of their time hunting for food. Each individual has its own special hunting ground, which it patrols during the evening and early morning hours. However, the ever hungry coyote is always looking for a meal. This is why *latrans* stops and investigates every badger hole it passes during the day. Rodents frequently take refuge in badger holes when the owners are out hunting.

Badgers are, from time to time, the unwilling partners of a hunting coyote. While the badger bores through the prickly-pear barricades that wood rats place around their nests, the coyote waits nearby and then seizes the rats as they flee. Hunting coyotes also make use of herds of grazing antelope, bison, and deer. Grasshoppers and mice are flushed by the feet of these animals, so coyotes following the herds are sure of a feast. Incidentally, some daring coyotes have learned that they will eat well if they follow bulldozers or hunt in cultivated fields under irrigation.

Coyotes may band together when hunting. The fastest of all canid runners, they join in chasing and pulling down deer. Two or more coyotes will also take turns chasing rabbits. When they do, the rabbits are driven in circles. This technique permits one coyote to pursue the prey while the others rest. From time to time, a refreshed coyote takes up the chase as the rabbit passes him. To overcome porcupines—which turn their heads on their attackers, spread their quills, and swish their heavily armed tails—a pair of coyotes alternate at making false charges.

Despite the fact that the artist who drew this picture over 125 years ago claimed it depicts an actual incident, it is probably totally imaginary. It is extremely unlikely that a pronghorn antelope doe and her fawn would stand watching a buck battle a pair of coyotes instead of galloping to safety.

Eventually, the porcupine fails to turn its back and one of the coyotes rushes in, jabs a paw under the chin, and flips its victim over on its back. The two coyotes then bite into the soft, unprotected belly.

Perhaps the most unusual hunting technique employed by a pair of coyotes is for one of them to run in circles, wave its tail, and leap up and down. Birds are fascinated by this display and, while they watch it, the other coyote sneaks up and secures lunch for two.

The wily coyote does not need a partner to be a successful hunter. One of its tricks is to destroy the dams that ground-

Although despised by many ranchers and hunters, latrans *is actually a good friend to man. The main dish on the menu of all subspecies of coyote are crop-destroying rodents such as the field mouse pictured here.*

dwelling rodents erect around their holes to keep out surface water. Then, remaining motionless in the rain, *latrans* waits for the drenched inhabitants of the burrows to come to the surface to avoid being drowned. When the rodents do come out, the coyote grabs them.

While stalking field mice, a coyote creeps slowly forward like a setter or a pointer seeking the scent of a game bird. With a foreleg raised off the ground, ears twitching, the hunter eases forward, putting each foot down softly, one after the other. When the rustle of a mouse is heard, the four feet are placed close together, the weight shifted backward, the muscles tightened. Then, suddenly, the body arches into the air and the two front paws come down on the mouse.

When attempting to drag down large prey, coyotes attack from the front, stabbing multiple wounds with their canines on the neck just behind the ears. While biting, the coyote braces its feet, hoping to check its prey's flight. Even if dragged, *latrans* holds on until it can grip the underside of the neck and sever the jugular vein.

Experienced lamb-killing coyotes crush their victims' heads, but individuals that have just begun to attack livestock lack this technique and bite anywhere they can. Raids on domestic stock usually occur just before dawn.

Social Organization

Song and legend celebrate the "lone coyote." However, *latrans* is quite social, often living in family groups consisting of a mated pair and their yearling offspring. Frequently, unattached adults of both sexes are also members of these clans.

The account of the habits of "prairie wolves" that accompanied this 125-year-old picture makes fascinating reading. Take for example: "On the banks of the Saskatchewan these animals start from the earth in great numbers on hearing the report of a gun, and gather round the hunter expectant of the offal of the animal he has slain."

63

But no pack of modern coyotes is as large as those that early travelers reported seeing on the Great Plains. Actually, these "packs" were really congregations of coyotes that had assembled to feed on buffalo carcasses.

Strict rules of conduct govern the relationship within a family group. Small individuals of both sexes give way to their larger kin, females are subservient to males, immatures obey all adults. In every family group there are a dominant male and female. Lower-ranking coyotes, particularly females, help rear the dominant pair's pups.

A coyote's rank is determined at a very early age. Pups fight and engage in ritual posing in order to establish their position in the hierarchy when about a month old. But once a high-

When about a month old, coyote pups begin to fight in order to establish their rank in the litter. Note the aggressive posture of the pup on the left (ears up, stiff gait) as it approaches a very submissive litter mate (ears flattened against the head, back arched in submissive display).

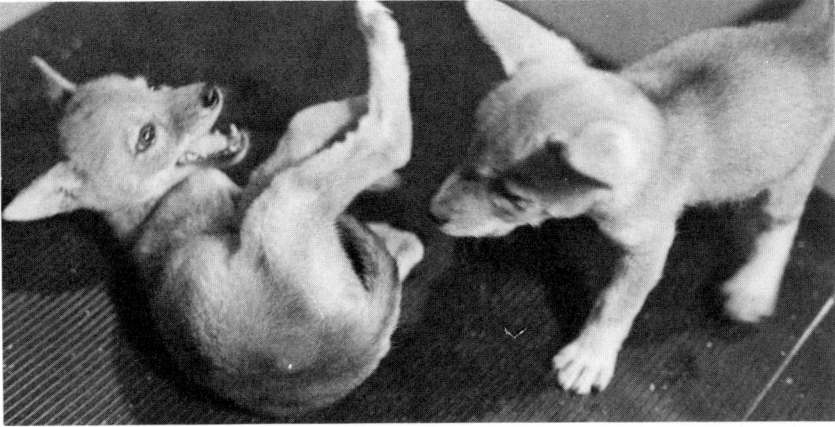

The pup on the left is acknowledging the dominance of its companion. By tucking its tail and forming the so-called "submissive grin" with its lips, the youngster avoids being bitten and mauled.

ranking coyote leaves its parents and litter mates, it is not automatically treated with respect by other coyotes it meets during its wanderings.

Pups of the year, on leaving their parents, soon discover that strange coyotes are not concerned with the rank a youngster held in a family group. This lesson is learned while a pup roams far and wide, seeking to find a territory it can mark out as its own. During its wanderings, a homeless coyote frequently enters the boundaries of established territories. It is the angry owner of such a territory that teaches the trespassing animal the unimportance of its former rank.

Although coyotes are constantly on the move, most of these encounters take place during the early evening when territories are being explored for food. As indicated, all coyotes have these hunting preserves (those of males being larger than those of females), which they guard zealously from trespassers. When confronted, intruders normally lower the hindquarters, arch the back, and hold the mouth open. This posture denotes

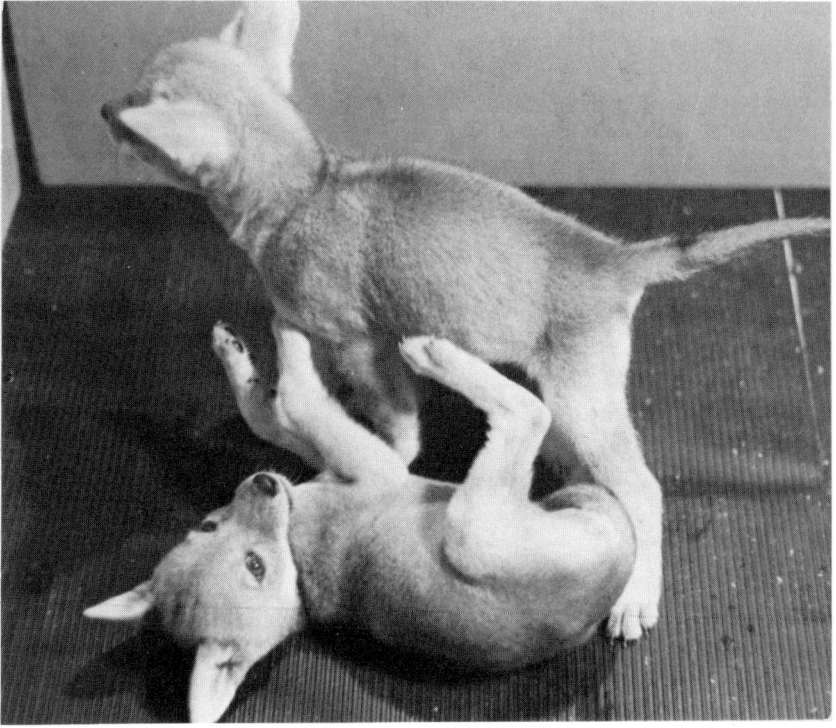

Once a pup's position in the hierarchy of a litter is determined, fighting between litter mates stops. As soon as a subservient pup assumes a submissive attitude, it is ignored by pups of higher rank.

submission and a desire to be friends. Sometimes the gesture is ignored and a fight ensues. But more often than not, after rolling the stranger over, placing the front paws on its chest, and growling a few times, the owner of the territory releases it.

Various ritual posings and different facial expressions stop most fights before they begin. Moreover, males are reluctant to attack females. Thus most of the fighting is between members of the same sex. Fights are preceded by the contestants' bristling of backs, baring of teeth, and holding the tail at the alert. After assuming this "threat position," the two rush at one another and circle like wary boxers, snapping and snarling. Eventually one animal admits defeat and slinks away.

The majority of fights occur during the winter when food is scarce and coyotes come from all directions to feed on large carcasses. While most individuals patiently await their turn, some of the assembly, driven by hunger and boldness, battle their way to the feast, driving away weaker diners. But despite this antisocial behavior, there are records of coyotes bringing food to others caught in traps. Healthy coyotes are also known to have provided care for sick and injured ones.

Raising a Family

Latrans' ability to survive despite destruction of habitat and widespread attempts to exterminate it is due in part to an ability to reproduce itself. Zoologists estimate that coyotes can triple their population in a year. However, observations have shown that if the coyote population in an area is using all available resources, the number of pups born will be just enough to replace the animals that have been killed or have died from natural causes. In years when the adult population has dropped appreciably, more pups are born.

Most coyotes mate for life or with the same individual several years in succession. But some males are polygamous. During their month-long courtship, coyotes hunt together, sing duets, and express affection by pawing and nuzzling one another.

Mated coyotes set up housekeeping in a den that is only used for whelping—adults normally sleep in sheltered spots. Dens can be anywhere—near a house, on the side of a cliff, under a pile of rocks, between roots, in a hollow tree or log, or in a culvert under a busy road. Usually, however, dens are underground. While coyotes may dig their own, they gladly sublet and enlarge burrows of foxes and other large ground-dwelling animals. *Latrans* is an excellent excavator, digging

Coyote at the entrance to its den. Evidently it has dragged its prey to the lair, which probably houses young.

with the front feet while pushing the soil backward out of the entrance of the den, where it forms a low, fan-shaped mound in front of the opening.

Underground dens consist of a tunnel one to two feet in diameter whose length, ranging from five to thirty feet, depends upon the texture of the soil. The tunnel ends in a chamber a little larger in height than the passageway. Sometimes two or more dens are prepared, and often the same den is used year after year. Males who have taken new mates may bring them to a den they have previously used, but the female always makes the final selection.

The breeding season for most subspecies begins in late January and ends in February, although environmental and weather factors influence whether or not coyotes whelp early or late. Young females usually whelp earlier than their elders. Thus when a mother and daughter share the same den—which is occasionally done by unrelated as well as related females—it contains two litters of different ages.

Gestation lasts approximately sixty-three days. While a litter of nineteen pups is known, the average is between five and seven. Pups are blind and helpless at birth. They are covered with short, woolly, dark or tawny-yellow hair. While the fur on the ears, back, and tail is quite dark, the fur on the underparts is pale.

Weighing about a pound at birth, coyote pups double that in a week. Active, they crawl around the whelping chamber, which contains no bedding and is kept clean by the female. Pups can walk at eight to ten days and are capable of running when a month old. The eyes open ten to fourteen days after

An unhappy coyote pup—it seems getting back on the ground isn't going to be nearly as much fun as was scrambling to the top of this huge rock.

Although only a pup, this youngster is as alert as any adult. Note the ears positioned to pick up the slightest sound, and the inquisitive look.

birth, and the pups start eating partially digested food regurgitated by their parents.

Coyotes are excellent parents. Not only do they cater to their offspring's every need but also they zealously guard them from danger. If adults feel their young are threatened or if a den becomes infested with fleas, the pups are moved to another location. Normally, this is near the original den. But one female is known to have carried her four pups, one at a time, to a new den five miles away, covering the forty miles in a single night!

As the pups grow, their appetites increase. Both parents supply them with regurgitated food. While the adults are away, the litter, which now makes daily excursions outside the den, awaits them anxiously. When the pups hear their parents calling, they run to them and satisfy their hunger. Before long, food is no longer regurgitated, the pups being given rodents and rabbits to dismember and eat at about a month in age. By the time they are nine weeks old, they are weaned.

Every day the curious pups wander greater distances from the den, dashing back to it when alarmed. Meanwhile, they learn to stalk grasshoppers and other insects. Both parents instruct the pups in the techniques of catching small game and familiarize them with edible vegetation.

In a very short time, the young of the year are competent foragers, hunters, and scavengers, capable of caring for themselves. Now, because their parents' territories contain a limited source of food, the youngsters must find hunting preserves of their own. To find one, certain individuals may be forced to trek a hundred miles if the area in which they were born has a large coyote population. However, as indicated, not all immatures disperse. Some remain with their parents, forming a family group. Eventually, some of these may leave, also.

Young coyotes in the wild, if they are fortunate, will find mates, raise families, and live for six to eight years. In contrast, coyotes in captivity may live as long as eighteen years.

This youngster is stalking a rodent. When he is near enough, he will pounce, stiff legged, on his victim.

"Decide no suit until you have heard both sides."
—PHOCYLIDES

5

MAN *vs.* COYOTE

Bears, mountain lions, and wolves prey on *latrans*, but far more coyotes die from disease and starvation than are killed by these natural enemies. However, the number of coyotes that suffer fatal illness or succumb to hunger is insignificant compared with the thousands destroyed by man. It has been estimated that at least 200,000 coyotes are shot, poisoned, and gassed every year.

The conflict between man and the coyote began when homesteaders unknowingly upset the balance of nature by bringing livestock and poultry into *latrans'* ancient hunting grounds. Always an opportunist, the intelligent coyote soon learned it was far easier to prey on cattle, poultry, and sheep than it was to stalk antelope, elk, or buffalo.

It would take several dozen books the size of this one to detail the controversy that has raged over the coyote's predatory activities during the last hundred years. Such an account would tell, among other things, of trappers releasing female coyotes in order to collect a bounty on their pups. There would also

There is good reason why the artists of the nineteenth century depicted the wolf (ABOVE) as being extremely vicious and made the coyote (RIGHT) seem to be a highly intelligent animal. The authors of the natural history books in which these pictures appeared maintained that the wolf was the "personification of ferocity" while its close kin the coyote was a "cowardly but cunning beast."

be descriptions of debates in Congress dealing with the question: "Should federal funds be spent to exterminate coyotes living on public land in order to insure sheepmen a profit?"

Originally, there was nothing to debate. Because coyotes preyed on domestic stock and wildlife, all agreed they should be destroyed. Today, we realize that coyotes and other predators are necessary to keep game populations within the limits of their habitat and food supply.

However, there are still those who are convinced that the only good coyote is a dead one. Most of these individuals are ranchers or sheepmen who would like their employees and the professional hunters and trappers working for the United States Government to use 1080. This deadly chemical compound was formerly injected into sheep carcasses to kill scavenging coyotes. Use of 1080 and other poisons on federal lands was barred by President Richard M. Nixon in 1972. Public pressure forced Nixon to take this action because 1080 was killing not only coyotes but badgers, foxes, eagles, and other creatures as well.

Meanwhile, the "coyote getter" was declared illegal. This weapon, triggered by a .38 cartridge, shot lethal sodium cyanide into a coyote's mouth when the animal tugged at the scented wool with which the device was baited. The M-44 replaced the "coyote getter." A spring-activated mechanism, it also expels cyanide into its victim's mouth. Although promoted as "a very selective control," the M-44 has killed not only bobcats, domestic and feral dogs, foxes, opossums, raccoons, and skunks but also is responsible for the death of a surveyor who accidentally tripped over one.

In recent years, authorities have become convinced that systematic poisoning on a large scale is no longer an economic and practical means of reducing the coyote population. Stockmen do not agree. Sheepmen in particular are sure that their industry will disappear unless coyotes are eliminated. Conser-

74

When sheep are not closely watched on rangeland, coyotes with a taste for lamb have little difficulty in satisfying their appetites. The sheep pictured here are being moved from one grazing ground in Nevada to another. The chances are they are being watched by coyotes.

vationists and environmentalists—who become quite emotional over the question of predator control—grant that *latrans* does prey on sheep but insist the damage done would be far less if sheep were managed better.

While conservationists and stockmen argue, hunters and wildlife experts wrangle. The hunters accuse *latrans* of killing game birds and fawns. While the conservationists admit this charge, they point out that coyotes weed out the unfit and keep the survivors alert. The coyote's defenders also remind the hunters that *latrans*, by preying on rabbits and vegetation-eating rodents, makes more grazing available for antelope, deer, and elk.

Meanwhile, there is a growing appreciation of all wildlife by the general public. Indeed, "for every person whose sheep may be molested by a coyote there are perhaps a thousand

who would thrill to hear a coyote chorus in the night." Thus there is now a concerted effort to find means of stopping coyote predation without the wholesale slaughter of thousands of animals. This endeavor is bolstered by scientific studies that show that only about twenty percent of all coyotes prey on domestic stock. But as yet no method has been devised that will destroy this small group and leave the rest of the coyote population unharmed.

Presently, researchers are seeking a chemical that, mixed with lamb, would make an animal vomit, thus conditioning any coyote that tasted the meat to avoid sheep. Other investigators are engaged in developing and designing a chemically treated collar for sheep that would discourage a coyote attack. Actually, a protective collar for sheep is not a new idea. Sears, Roebuck advertised such a sheep collar (containing no poison) in its catalog at the turn of the century!

Hopefully, some means of controlling coyote predation pleasing to both conservationists and stockmen will be developed. Meanwhile, despite persecution, there is little chance that the coyote will be exterminated. Laurence Pringle, an authority on predator ecology and behavior, has made this clear. According to Pringle, "If the federal predator control program is regarded as a war, humans can claim only partial, local victories, while the coyote continues to reign over the main battlefield."

In other words, *latrans* is too adaptable, cunning, and intelligent to be destroyed by its worst enemy—man.

Past efforts at coyote-proof fencing failed because all the wires in the fences were charged. As a result, fence-climbing coyotes, not being grounded, did not receive a shock. The fence shown here alternates electrified and ground wires from top to bottom, making it impossible for a predator to avoid simultaneous contact with a charged and a ground wire. The shock—generated by a battery—repels but does not injure coyotes, dogs, or sheep that come in contact with the fence.

Index

80